HAL LEONARD STUDENT PIANO LIBRARY

INTERMEDIATE

Piano Recital Showcase

T0086585

CHRISTMAS EVE SOLOS

10 CHRISTMAS FAVORITES

ISBN 978-1-4584-1183-9

HAL•LEONARD®
CORPORATION
7777 W. BLUEMOUND RD. P.O. BOX 13819 MILWAUKEE, WI 53213

In Australia Contact:
Hal Leonard Australia Pty. Ltd.
4 Lentara Court
Cheltenham, Victoria, 3192 Australia
Email: ausadmin@halleonard.com.au

Visit Hal Leonard Online at
www.halleonard.com

CONTENTS

Bring a Torch, Jeanette, Isabella

17th Century French Provençal Carol
Arranged by Carol Klose

Both hands 8va the first time through.

Bring a torch, ___ Jean-
Has - ten now, ___ good

nette, Is - a - bel - la, Bring a torch, ___ come swift - ly and
folk of the vil - lage, Has - ten now, ___ the Christ Child to

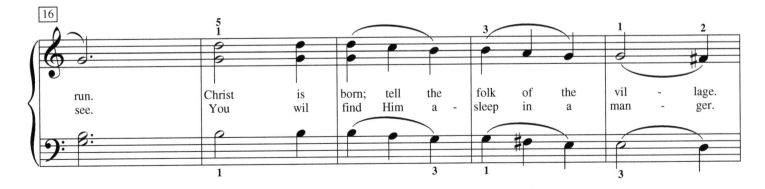

run. Christ is born; tell the folk of the vil - lage.
see. You wil find Him a - sleep in a man - ger.

Je - sus is sleep - ing in His cra - dle. Ah,
Qui - et - ly come and in whis - per cra - dle. Hush,
poco rit.
mp *a tempo*

ah, Beau - ti - ful is the Moth - er. Ah,
hush, Peace - ful - ly now He slum - bers. Hush,

1.
ah, Beau - ti - ful is her Son. _____
hush, Peace - ful - ly

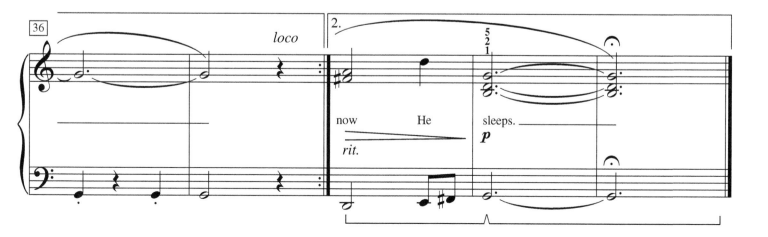

loco 2.
now He sleeps. _____
p
rit.

Coventry Carol

Words by Robert Croo
Traditional English Melody
Arranged by Jennifer Linn

Andante cantabile (♩ = 66)

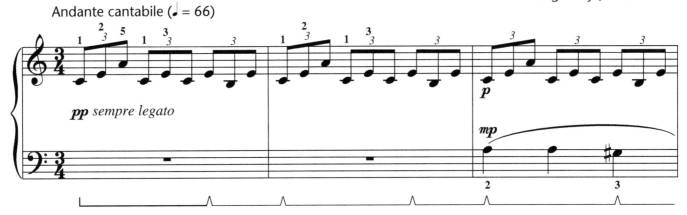

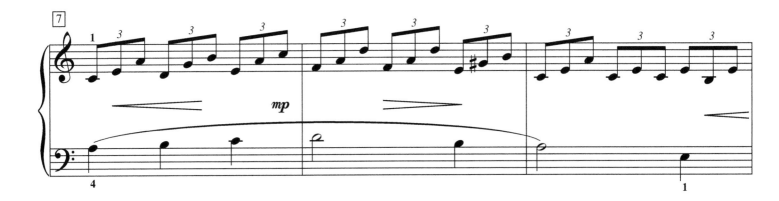

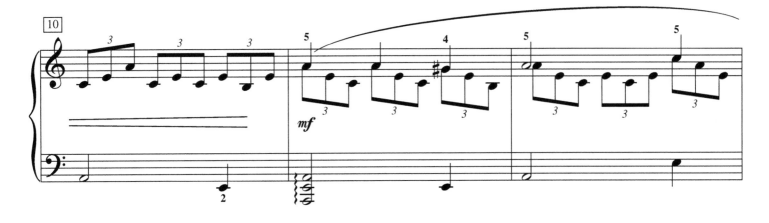

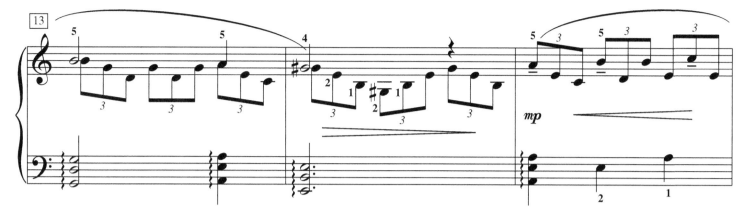

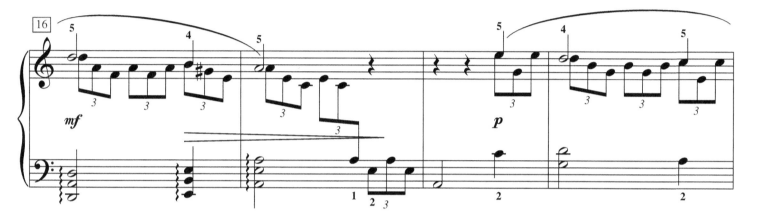

O Little Town of Bethlehem

Words by Phillips Brooks
Music by Lewis H. Redner
Arranged by Mona Rejino

Gently, with expression (♩ = 88)

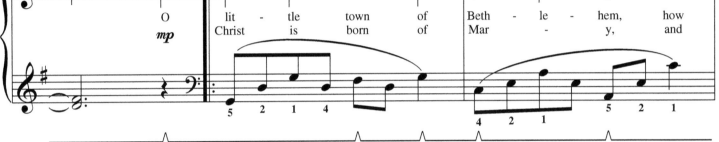

Second time both hands 8va

O lit - tle town of Beth - le - hem, how
Christ is born of Mar - - y, and

still we ___ see thee lie. A - bove thy deep and
gath - ered ___ all a - bove, while mor - tals deep sleep, the

Second time loco

dream - less sleep the si - lent ___ stars go by. Yet O
an - gels keep their watch of ___ won - d'ring love.

9

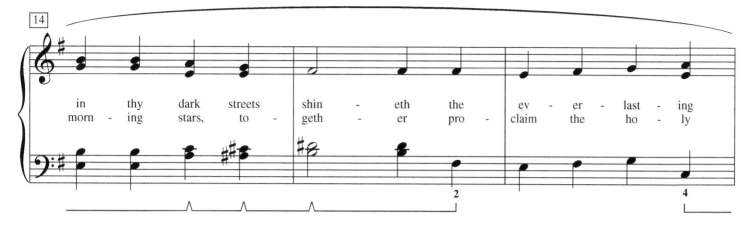

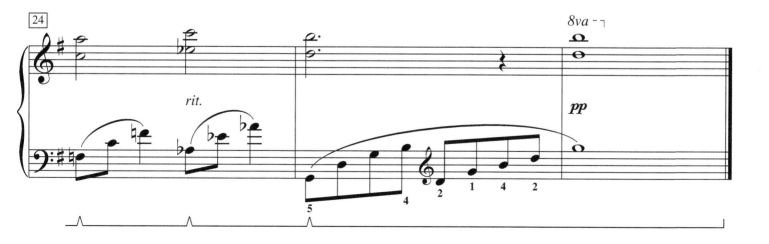

Silent Night

Music by Franz Gruber
Arranged by Mike Springer

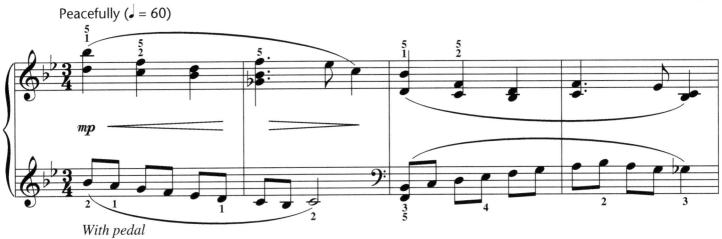

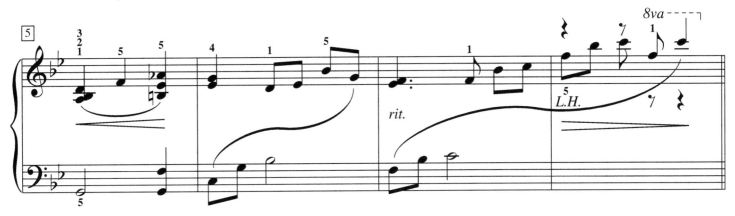

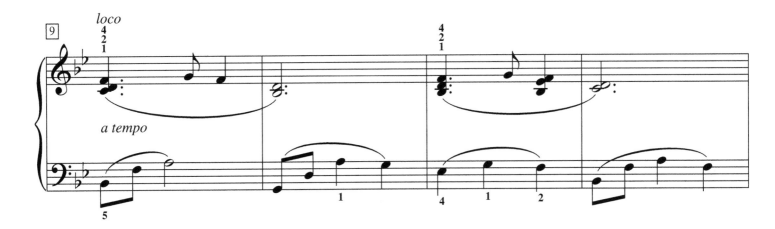

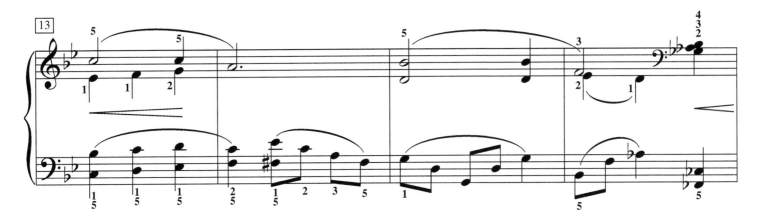

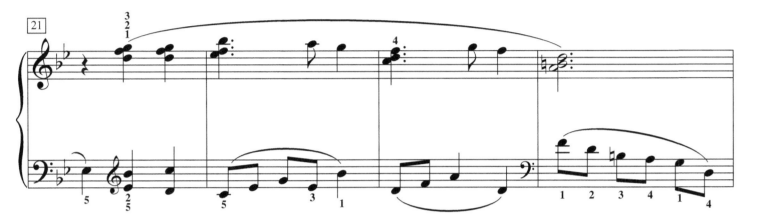

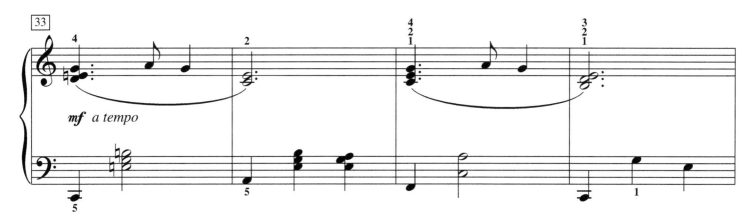

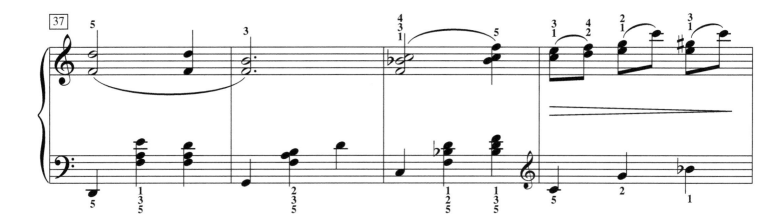

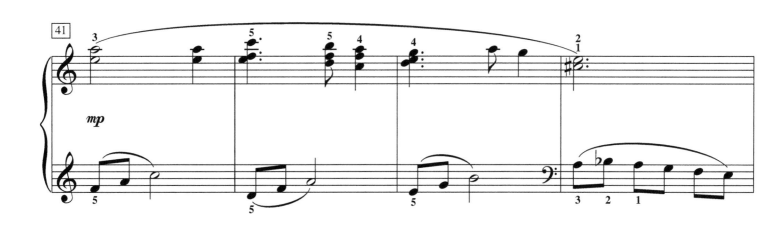

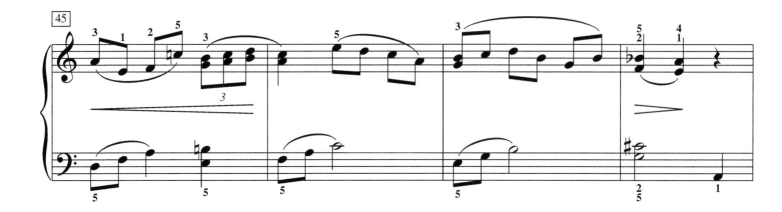

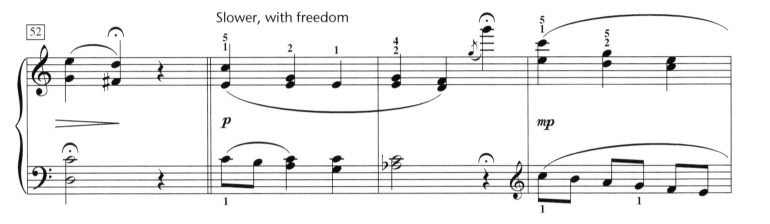

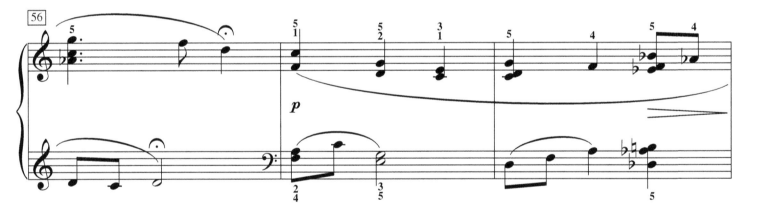

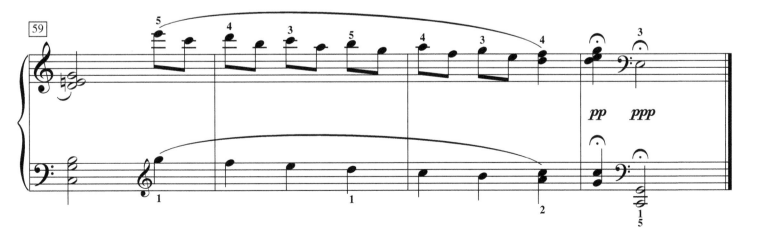

Shepherd's Dream

By Carol Klose

With feeling (♩ = 108-116)

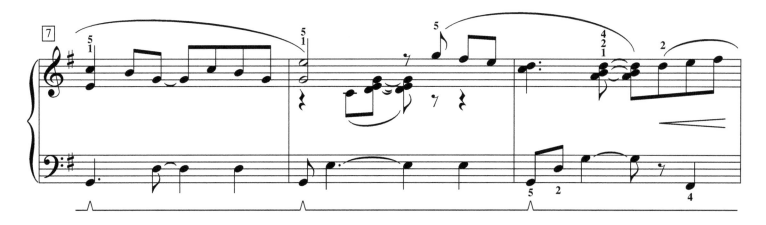

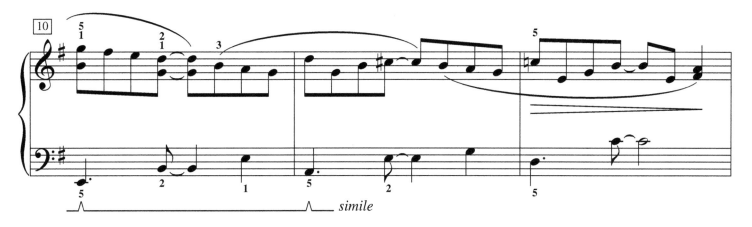

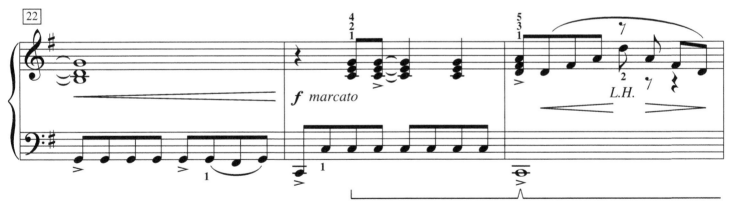

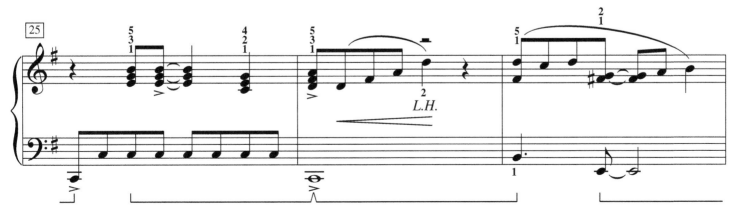

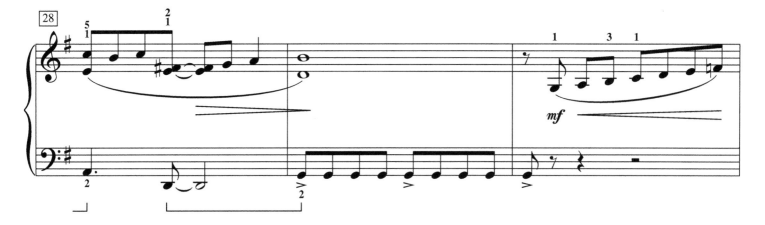

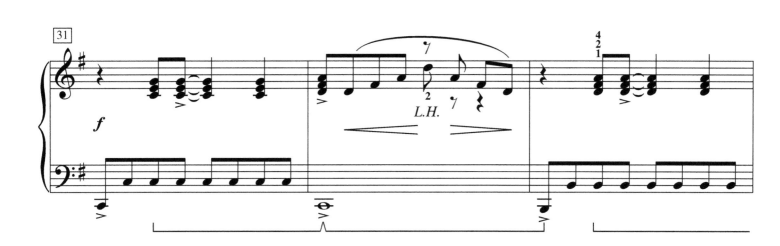

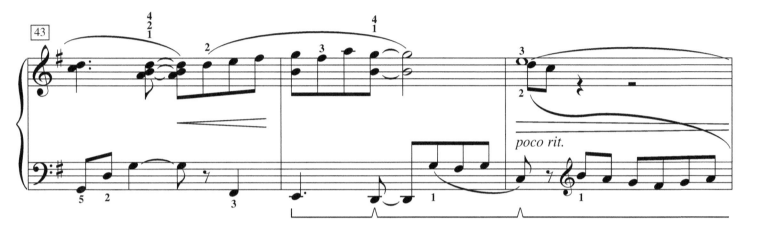

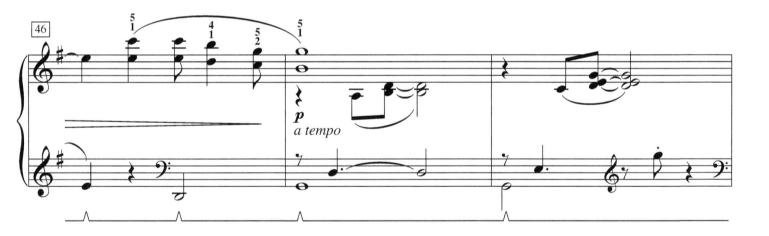

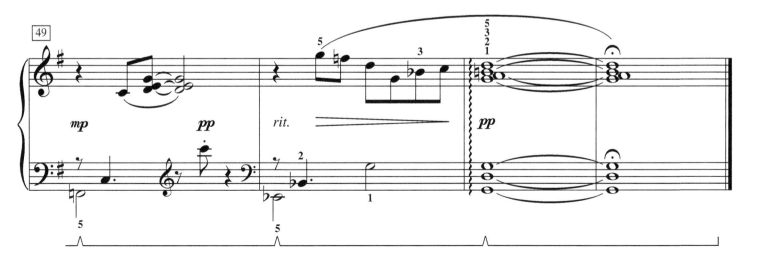

Auld Lang Syne

Words by Robert Burns
Traditional Scottish Melody
Arranged by Phillip Keveren

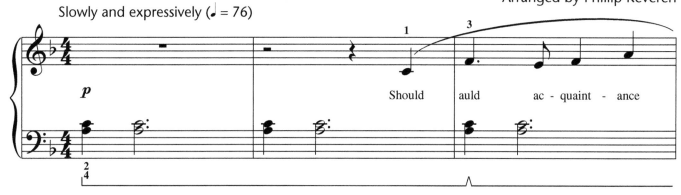

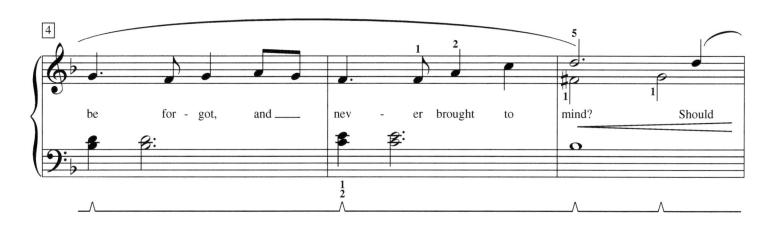

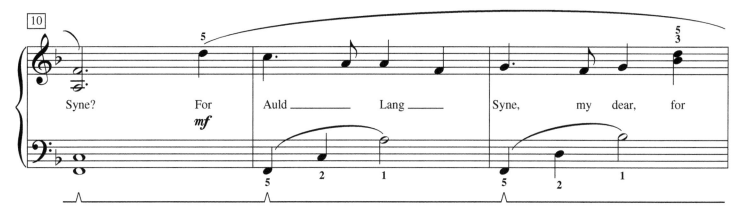

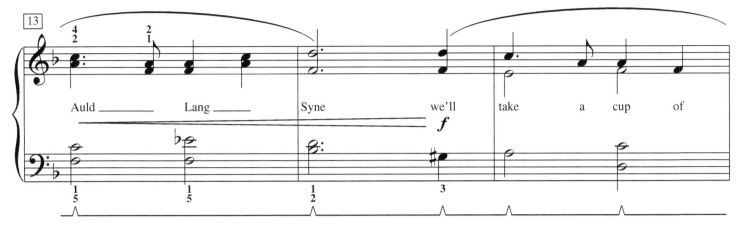

Auld _____ Lang _____ Syne we'll take a cup of

kind - ness yet for ___ Auld _____ Lang ___ Syne.

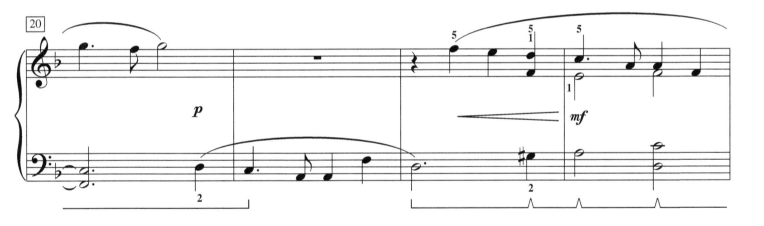

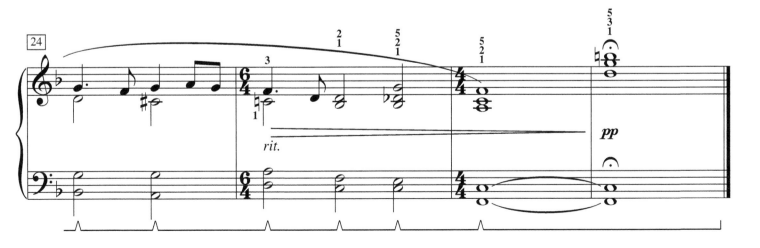

We Wish You a Merry Christmas

Traditional English Carol
Arranged by Mike Springer

Jazz Waltz (♩ = 120-132)

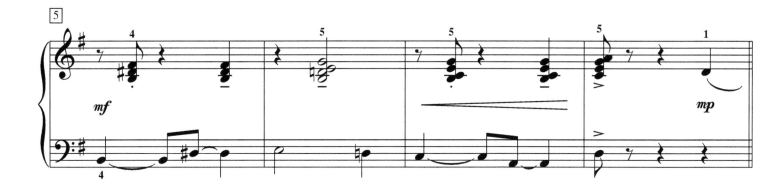

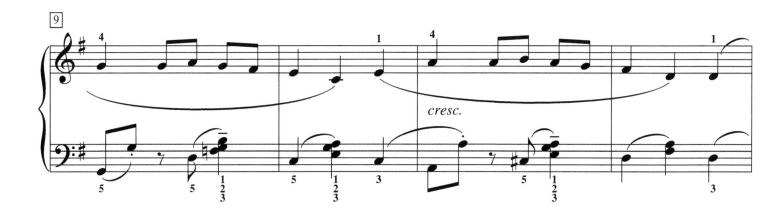

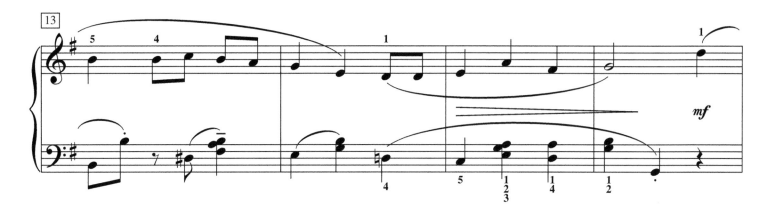

21

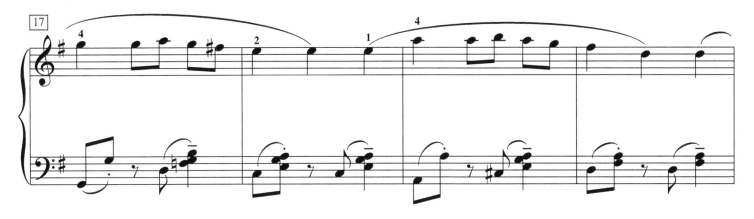

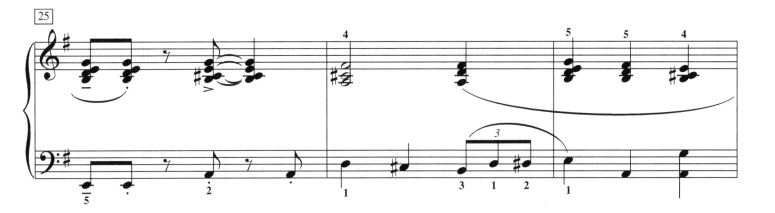

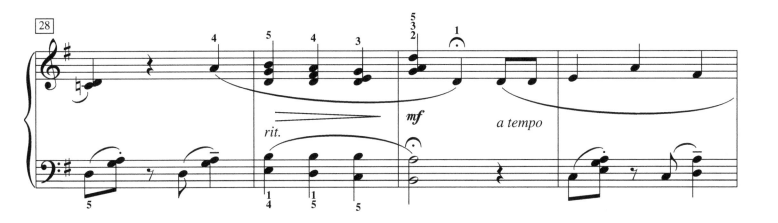

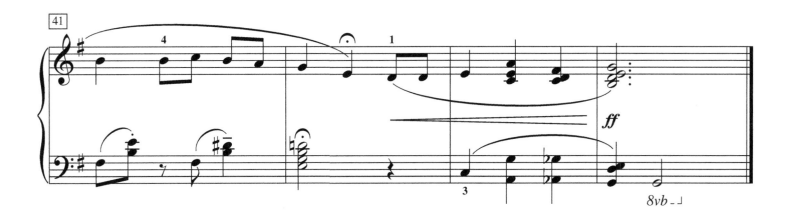

MEDLEYS

Christmas Fantasia

By Jennifer Linn

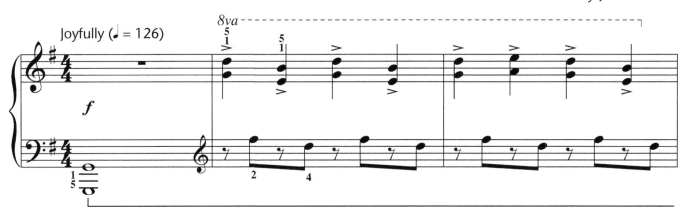

"O Come, All Ye Faithful"
Music by John Francis Wade
Latin Words translated by Frederick Oakeley

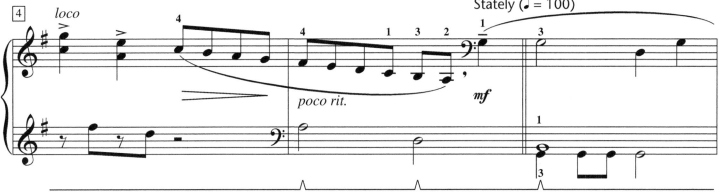

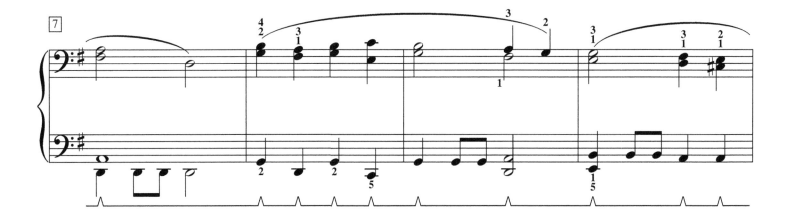

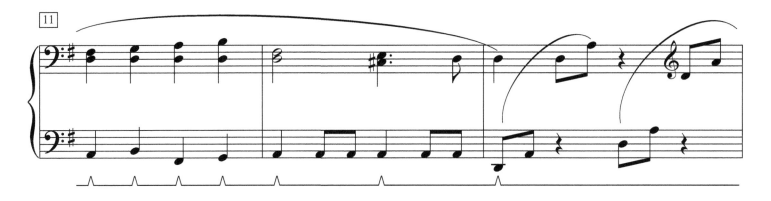

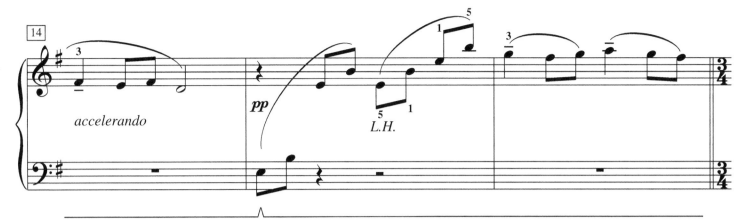

accelerando

pp

L.H.

"Ukrainian Bell Carol"
Traditional
Allegro molto (♩ = 168)

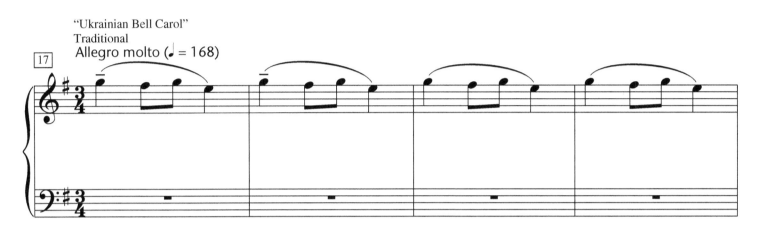

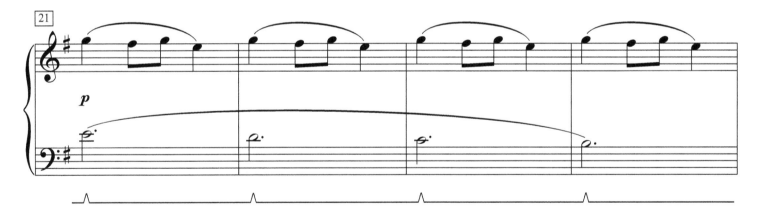

p

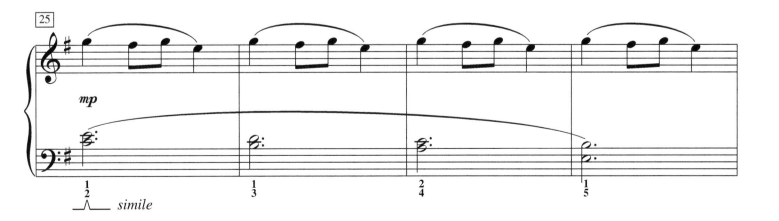

mp

simile

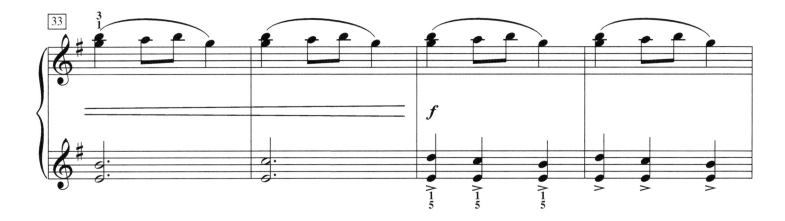

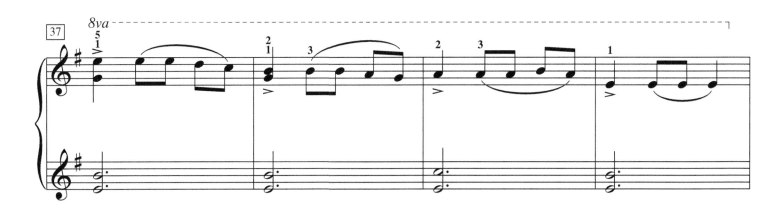

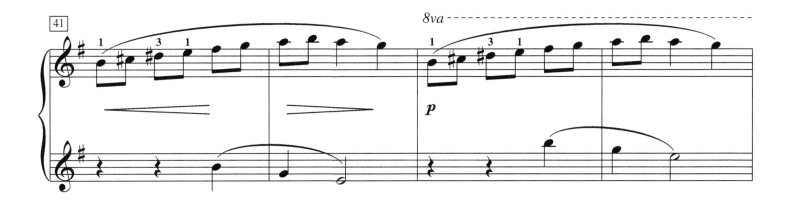

"God Rest Ye Merry, Gentlemen"
19th Century English Carol
Andante, with dignity (♩ = 104)

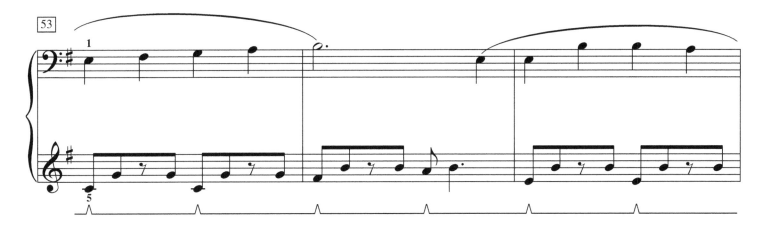

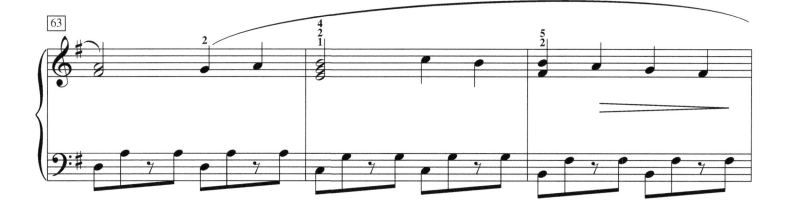

"Joy to the World"
Words by Isaac Watts
Music by George Frideric Handel
Adapted by Lowell Mason

Joyously (♩ = 126)

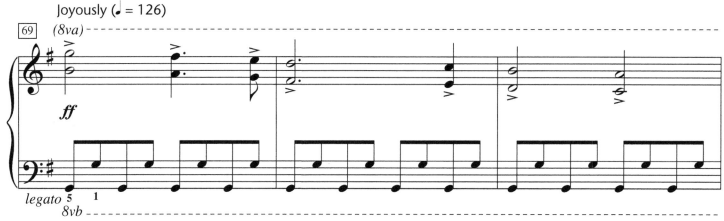

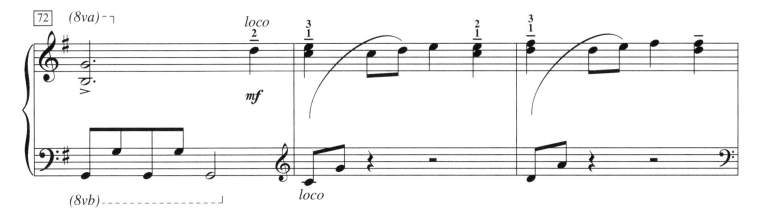

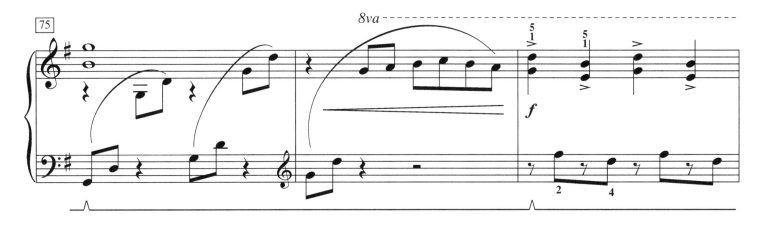

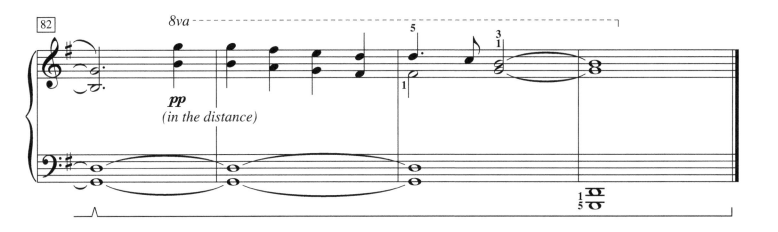

Good News Medley

Mary Had a Baby • Go, Tell It on the Mountain

Arranged by Mona Rejino

Moderately slow Swing ($\sqcap$ = $\downarrow$ $\downarrow$) ($\downarrow$ = 92)

"Mary Had a Baby"
(African-American Spiritual)

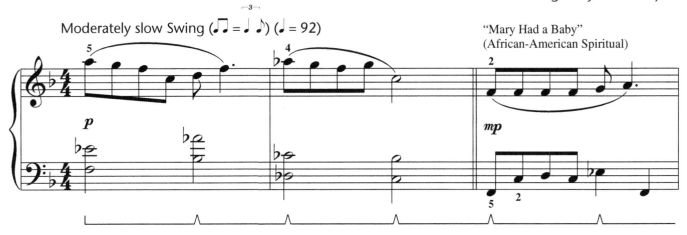

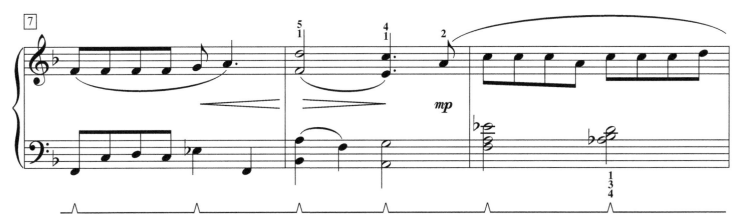

32

"Go, Tell It on the Mountain" (African-American Spiritual)

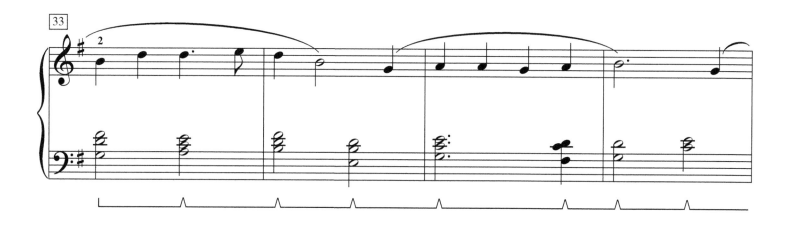

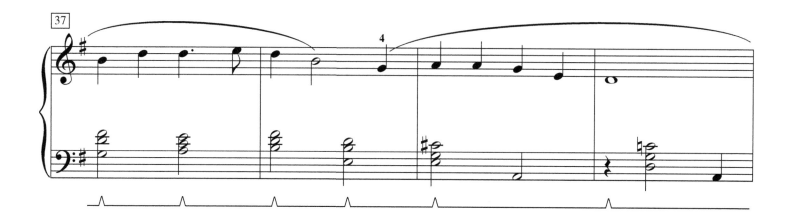

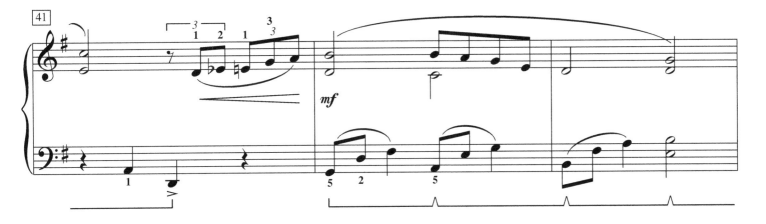

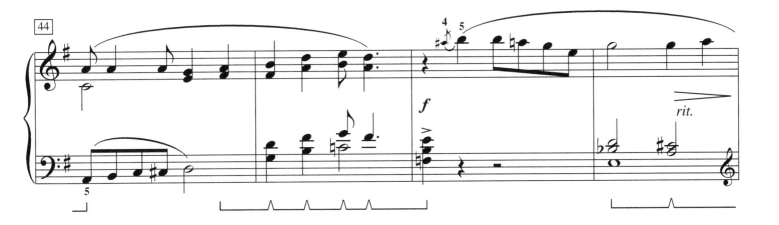

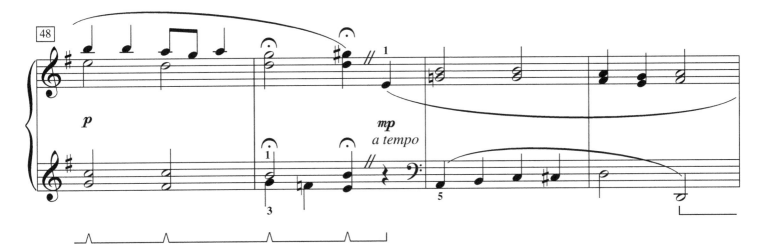

To Christian James

So Tender and Mild
A Christmas Medley

By Phillip Keveren

Sweetly (♩ = 88)

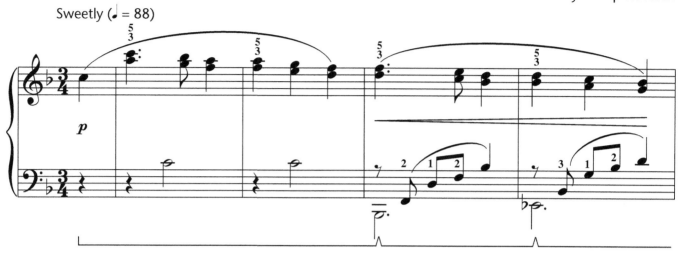

Flowing (♩ =110)

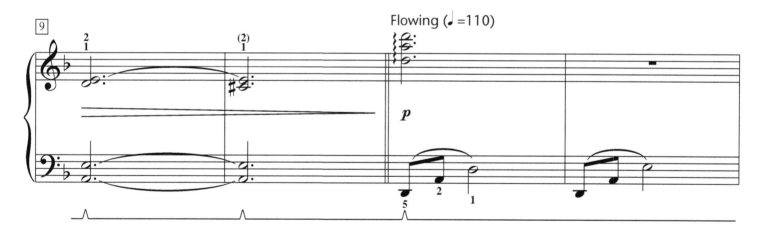

"We Three Kings" (J.H. Hopkins, Jr.)

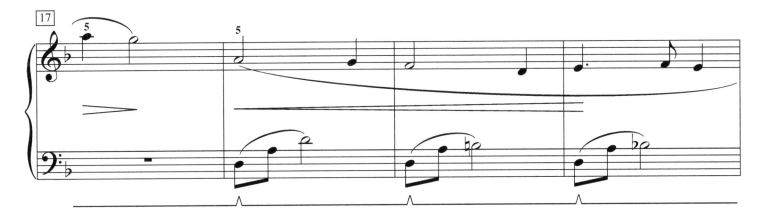

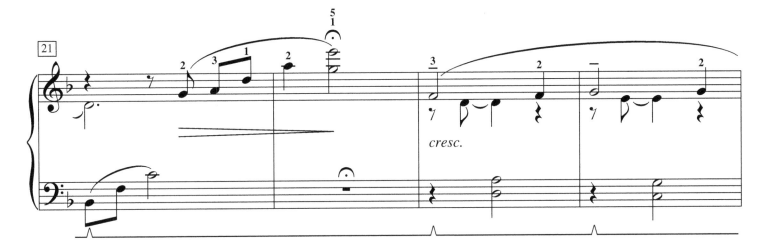

Gently (♩ = 96)

"It Came Upon the Midnight Clear" (R.S. Willis)

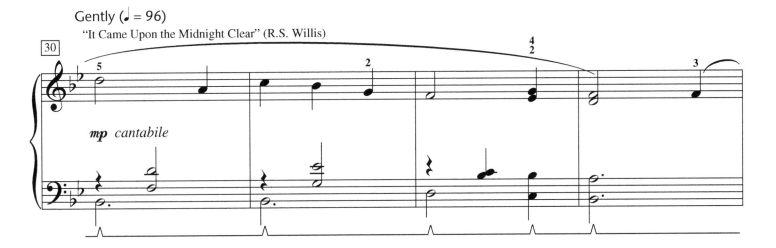

Slowly, freely (♩ ca. 80)
"The Coventry Carol" (15th Century English)

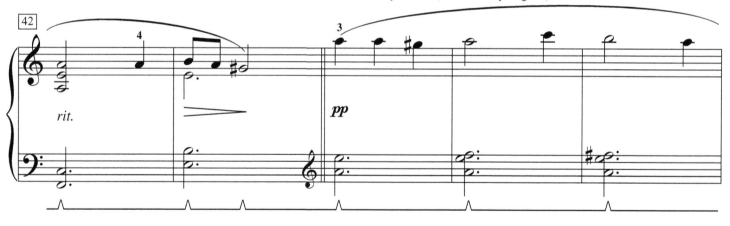

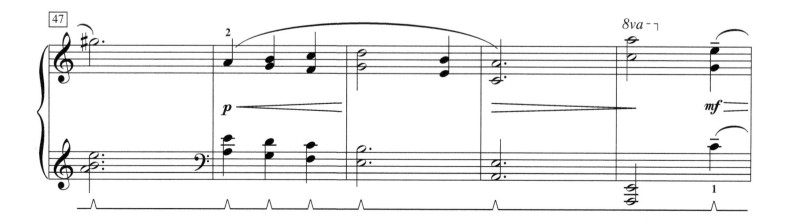

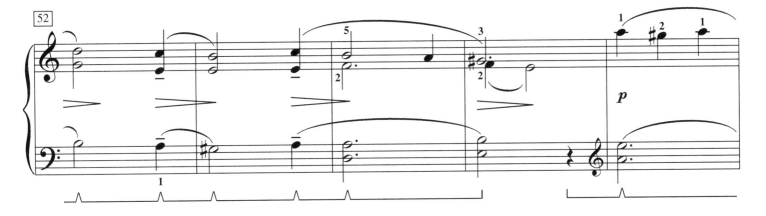

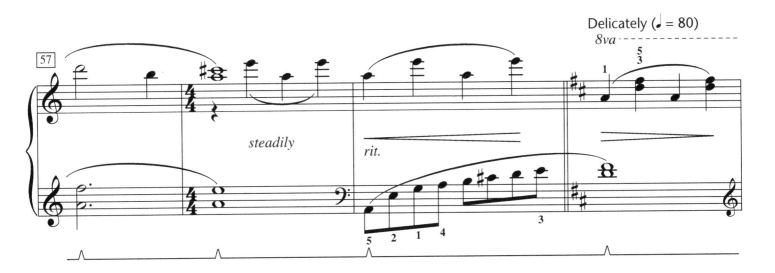

"Still, Still, Still" (Austrian Carol)

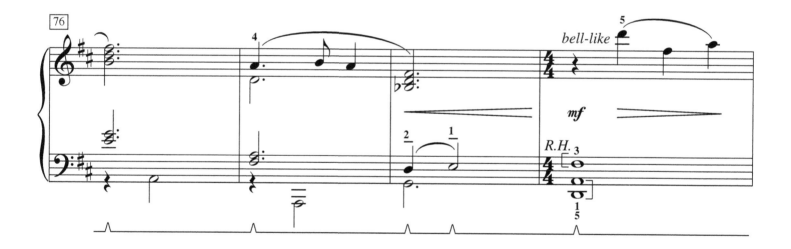

POPULAR SONGS
HAL LEONARD STUDENT PIANO LIBRARY

The **Hal Leonard Student Piano Library** has great songs, and you will find all your favorites here: Disney classics, Broadway and movie favorites, and today's top hits. These graded collections are skillfully and imaginatively arranged for students and pianists at every level, from elementary solos with teacher accompaniments to sophisticated piano solos for the advancing pianist.

Adele
arr. Mona Rejino
Correlates with HLSPL Level 5
00159590..............................$12.99

The Beatles
arr. Eugénie Rocherolle
Correlates with HLSPL Level 5
00296649..............................$12.99

Irving Berlin Piano Duos
arr. Don Heitler and Jim Lyke
Correlates with HLSPL Level 5
00296838..............................$14.99

Broadway Favorites
arr. Phillip Keveren
Correlates with HLSPL Level 4
00279192..............................$12.99

Chart Hits
arr. Mona Rejino
Correlates with HLSPL Level 5
00296710..............................$8.99

Christmas at the Piano
arr. Lynda Lybeck-Robinson
Correlates with HLSPL Level 4
00298194..............................$12.99

Christmas Cheer
arr. Phillip Keveren
Correlates with HLSPL Level 4
00296616..............................$8.99

Classic Christmas Favorites
arr. Jennifer & Mike Watts
Correlates with HLSPL Level 5
00129582..............................$9.99

Christmas Time Is Here
arr. Eugénie Rocherolle
Correlates with HLSPL Level 5
00296614..............................$8.99

Classic Joplin Rags
arr. Fred Kern
Correlates with HLSPL Level 5
00296743..............................$9.99

Classical Pop – Lady Gaga Fugue & Other Pop Hits
arr. Giovanni Dettori
Correlates with HLSPL Level 5
00296921..............................$12.99

Contemporary Movie Hits
arr. by Carol Klose, Jennifer Linn and Wendy Stevens
Correlates with HLSPL Level 5
00296780..............................$8.99

Contemporary Pop Hits
arr. Wendy Stevens
Correlates with HLSPL Level 3
00296836..............................$8.99

Cool Pop
arr. Mona Rejino
Correlates with HLSPL Level 5
00360103..............................$12.99

Country Favorites
arr. Mona Rejino
Correlates with HLSPL Level 5
00296861..............................$9.99

Disney Favorites
arr. Phillip Keveren
Correlates with HLSPL Levels 3/4
00296647..............................$10.99

Disney Film Favorites
arr. Mona Rejino
Correlates with HLSPL Level 5
00296809 ....$10.99

Disney Piano Duets
arr. Jennifer & Mike Watts
Correlates with HLSPL Level 5
00113759..............................$13.99

Double Agent! Piano Duets
arr. Jeremy Siskind
Correlates with HLSPL Level 5
00121595..............................$12.99

Easy Christmas Duets
arr. Mona Rejino & Phillip Keveren
Correlates with HLSPL Levels 3/4
00237139..............................$9.99

Easy Disney Duets
arr. Jennifer and Mike Watts
Correlates with HLSPL Level 4
00243727..............................$12.99

Four Hands on Broadway
arr. Fred Kern
Correlates with HLSPL Level 5
00146177..............................$12.99

Frozen Piano Duets
arr. Mona Rejino
Correlates with HLSPL Levels 3/4
00144294..............................$12.99

Hip-Hop for Piano Solo
arr. Logan Evan Thomas
Correlates with HLSPL Level 5
00360950..............................$12.99

Jazz Hits for Piano Duet
arr. Jeremy Siskind
Correlates with HLSPL Level 5
00143248..............................$12.99

Elton John
arr. Carol Klose
Correlates with HLSPL Level 5
00296721..............................$10.99

Joplin Ragtime Duets
arr. Fred Kern
Correlates with HLSPL Level 5
00296771..............................$8.99

Movie Blockbusters
arr. Mona Rejino
Correlates with HLSPL Level 5
00232850..............................$10.99

The Nutcracker Suite
arr. Lynda Lybeck-Robinson
Correlates with HLSPL Levels 3/4
00147906..............................$8.99

Pop Hits for Piano Duet
arr. Jeremy Siskind
Correlates with HLSPL Level 5
00224734..............................$12.99

Sing to the King
arr. Phillip Keveren
Correlates with HLSPL Level 5
00296808..............................$8.99

Smash Hits
arr. Mona Rejino
Correlates with HLSPL Level 5
00284841..............................$10.99

Spooky Halloween Tunes
arr. Fred Kern
Correlates with HLSPL Levels 3/4
00121550..............................$9.99

Today's Hits
arr. Mona Rejino
Correlates with HLSPL Level 5
00296646..............................$9.99

Top Hits
arr. Jennifer and Mike Watts
Correlates with HLSPL Level 5
00296894..............................$10.99

Top Piano Ballads
arr. Jennifer Watts
Correlates with HLSPL Level 5
00197926..............................$10.99

Video Game Hits
arr. Mona Rejino
Correlates with HLSPL Level 4
00300310..............................$12.99

You Raise Me Up
arr. Deborah Brady
Correlates with HLSPL Level 2/3
00296576..............................$7.95

HAL•LEONARD®
7777 W. BLUEMOUND RD. P.O. BOX 13819 MILWAUKEE, WI 53213

Prices, contents and availability subject to change without notice. Prices may vary outside the U.S.

Visit our website at www.halleonard.com

COMPOSER SHOWCASE
HAL LEONARD STUDENT PIANO LIBRARY

This series showcases great original piano music from our **Hal Leonard Student Piano Library** family of composers. Carefully graded for easy selection.

BILL BOYD

JAZZ BITS (AND PIECES)
Early Intermediate Level
00290312 11 Solos......................$7.99

JAZZ DELIGHTS
Intermediate Level
00240435 11 Solos......................$8.99

JAZZ FEST
Intermediate Level
00240436 10 Solos......................$8.99

JAZZ PRELIMS
Early Elementary Level
00290032 12 Solos......................$7.99

JAZZ SKETCHES
Intermediate Level
00220001 8 Solos........................$8.99

JAZZ STARTERS
Elementary Level
00290425 10 Solos......................$8.99

JAZZ STARTERS II
Late Elementary Level
00290434 11 Solos......................$7.99

JAZZ STARTERS III
Late Elementary Level
00290465 12 Solos......................$8.99

THINK JAZZ!
Early Intermediate Level
00290417 Method Book............$12.99

TONY CARAMIA

JAZZ MOODS
Intermediate Level
00296728 8 Solos........................$6.95

SUITE DREAMS
Intermediate Level
00296775 4 Solos........................$6.99

SONDRA CLARK

DAKOTA DAYS
Intermediate Level
00296521 5 Solos........................$6.95

FLORIDA FANTASY SUITE
Intermediate Level
00296766 3 Duets........................$7.95

THREE ODD METERS
Intermediate Level
00296472 3 Duets........................$6.95

MATTHEW EDWARDS

CONCERTO FOR YOUNG PIANISTS
FOR 2 PIANOS, FOUR HANDS
Intermediate Level Book/CD
00296356 3 Movements $19.99

CONCERTO NO. 2 IN G MAJOR
FOR 2 PIANOS, 4 HANDS
Intermediate Level Book/CD
00296670 3 Movements............$17.99

PHILLIP KEVEREN

MOUSE ON A MIRROR
Late Elementary Level
00296361 5 Solos........................$8.99

MUSICAL MOODS
Elementary/Late Elementary Level
00296714 7 Solos........................$6.99

SHIFTY-EYED BLUES
Late Elementary Level
00296374 5 Solos........................$7.99

CAROL KLOSE

THE BEST OF CAROL KLOSE
Early to Late Intermediate Level
00146151 15 Solos....................$12.99

CORAL REEF SUITE
Late Elementary Level
00296354 7 Solos........................$7.50

DESERT SUITE
Intermediate Level
00296667 6 Solos........................$7.99

FANCIFUL WALTZES
Early Intermediate Level
00296473 5 Solos........................$7.95

GARDEN TREASURES
Late Intermediate Level
00296787 5 Solos........................$8.50

ROMANTIC EXPRESSIONS
Intermediate to Late Intermediate Level
00296923 5 Solos........................$8.99

WATERCOLOR MINIATURES
Early Intermediate Level
00296848 7 Solos........................$7.99

JENNIFER LINN

AMERICAN IMPRESSIONS
Intermediate Level
00296471 6 Solos........................$8.99

ANIMALS HAVE FEELINGS TOO
Early Elementary/Elementary Level
00147789 8 Solos........................$8.99

AU CHOCOLAT
Late Elementary/Early Intermediate Level
00298110 7 Solos........................$8.99

CHRISTMAS IMPRESSIONS
Intermediate Level
00296706 8 Solos........................$8.99

JUST PINK
Elementary Level
00296722 9 Solos........................$8.99

LES PETITES IMAGES
Late Elementary Level
00296664 7 Solos........................$8.99

LES PETITES IMPRESSIONS
Intermediate Level
00296355 6 Solos........................$8.99

REFLECTIONS
Late Intermediate Level
00296843 5 Solos........................$8.99

TALES OF MYSTERY
Intermediate Level
00296769 6 Solos........................$8.99

LYNDA LYBECK-ROBINSON

ALASKA SKETCHES
Early Intermediate Level
00119637 8 Solos........................$8.99

AN AWESOME ADVENTURE
Late Elementary Level
00137563 8 Solos........................$7.99

FOR THE BIRDS
Early Intermediate/Intermediate Level
00237078 9 Solos........................$8.99

WHISPERING WOODS
Late Elementary Level
00275905 9 Solos........................$8.99

MONA REJINO

CIRCUS SUITE
Late Elementary Level
00296665 5 Solos........................$8.99

COLOR WHEEL
Early Intermediate Level
00201951 6 Solos........................$9.99

IMPRESIONES DE ESPAÑA
Intermediate Level
00337520 6 Solos........................$8.99

IMPRESSIONS OF NEW YORK
Intermediate Level
00364212.....................................$8.99

JUST FOR KIDS
Elementary Level
00296840 8 Solos........................$7.99

MERRY CHRISTMAS MEDLEYS
Intermediate Level
00296799 5 Solos........................$8.99

MINIATURES IN STYLE
Intermediate Level
00148088 6 Solos........................$8.99

PORTRAITS IN STYLE
Early Intermediate Level
00296507 6 Solos........................$8.99

EUGÉNIE ROCHEROLLE

CELEBRATION SUITE
Intermediate Level
00152724 3 Duets........................$8.99

ENCANTOS ESPAÑOLES (SPANISH DELIGHTS)
Intermediate Level
00125451 6 Solos........................$8.99

JAMBALAYA
Intermediate Level
00296654 2 Pianos, 8 Hands.....$12.99
00296725 2 Pianos, 4 Hands.......$7.95

JEROME KERN CLASSICS
Intermediate Level
00296577 10 Solos....................$12.99

LITTLE BLUES CONCERTO
Early Intermediate Level
00142801 2 Pianos, 4 Hands......$12.99

TOUR FOR TWO
Late Elementary Level
00296832 6 Duets........................$9.99

TREASURES
Late Elementary/Early Intermediate Level
00296924 7 Solos........................$8.99

JEREMY SISKIND

BIG APPLE JAZZ
Intermediate Level
00278209 8 Solos........................$8.99

MYTHS AND MONSTERS
Late Elementary/Early Intermediate Level
00148148 9 Solos........................$8.99

CHRISTOS TSITSAROS

DANCES FROM AROUND THE WORLD
Early Intermediate Level
00296688 7 Solos........................$8.99

FIVE SUMMER PIECES
Late Intermediate/Advanced Level
00361235 5 Solos......................$12.99

LYRIC BALLADS
Intermediate/Late Intermediate Level
00102404 6 Solos........................$8.99

POETIC MOMENTS
Intermediate Level
00296403 8 Solos........................$8.99

SEA DIARY
Early Intermediate Level
00253486 9 Solos........................$8.99

SONATINA HUMORESQUE
Late Intermediate Level
00296772 3 Movements.............$6.99

SONGS WITHOUT WORDS
Intermediate Level
00296506 9 Solos........................$9.99

THREE PRELUDES
Early Advanced Level
00130747 3 Solos........................$8.99

THROUGHOUT THE YEAR
Late Elementary Level
00296723 12 Duets.....................$6.95

ADDITIONAL COLLECTIONS

AT THE LAKE
by Elvina Pearce
Elementary/Late Elementary Level
00131642 10 Solos and Duets.....$7.99

CHRISTMAS FOR TWO
by Dan Fox
Early Intermediate Level
00290069 13 Duets....................$8.99

CHRISTMAS JAZZ
by Mike Springer
Intermediate Level
00296525 6 Solos........................$8.99

COUNTY RAGTIME FESTIVAL
by Fred Kern
Intermediate Level
00296882 7 Solos........................$7.99

LITTLE JAZZERS
by Jennifer Watts
Elementary/Late Elementary Level
00154573 9 Solos........................$8.99

PLAY THE BLUES!
by Luann Carman
Early Intermediate Level
00296357 10 Solos.....................$9.99

ROLLER COASTERS & RIDES
by Jennifer & Mike Watts
Intermediate Level
00131144 8 Duets........................$8.99

www.halleonard.com

Prices, contents, and availability subject to change without notice.